BLOCK PORN

Not so simple way to quit porn. Willpower is never enough.

RYAN SANDERS

TABLE OF CONTENT

INTRODUCTION

Pornography was always that aspect of my life that I had to keep hidden from potential romantic partners, and it was starting to chip away at my moral fiber.

I transitioned from sensual photographs to softcore porn to hardcore porn to erotic twerking videos to incest videos (even if I never considered acting this one out); I even looked into transgender porn (I'm straight AF). To get the amount of enjoyment I desired, I had to keep exploring deeper things to explore. I eventually began visiting brothels to partake in what I had been seeing. I had become a shell of my former self because of porn.

I used to be an active adolescent before I got into porn. I loved spending time with my friends, I was active in athletics, and I was kind of like the "Alpha male" among my friends. As a small-framed man in high school, I recall chatting to females without any difficulty. I wasn't afraid to approach women.

My issue began when I was 15 years old and one of my buddies showed us porn from waptrick.com. When I saw it, it stuck. After receiving my phone a few months later, things started to go south.

Thankfully, using the techniques I'm going to uncover in this book, I've been able to eliminate pornography from my life. Though challenging, the effort was worthwhile.

Realizing that you are hooked is the first step to recovery. The next is to do all in your power to stop the problem before it destroys your life. Porn causes you to behave in ways that make you wonder whether you are already mentally unstable. To assist parents, singles, and even children in limiting their access to pornography on Android phones, the book Quit Porn: Guide to Block Porn from Your Android Phone was developed. According to research with over 10,000 replies, willpower can only go so far in helping someone overcome porn addiction. Without a suitable strategy to prevent access to it, there is a strong likelihood that one's efforts to recuperate will be unsuccessful.

You may discover detailed instructions on how to configure your phone's programs to protect yourself from porn. This should assist, along with your will and willpower to stop watching porn.

PORN ADDICTION

You could question whether you have a porn addiction if you are unable to put down your device, even when you have work to do, supper to cook, the dog to walk, or your 10th wedding anniversary to celebrate with your beloved. And you could believe you do if this insatiable yearning is producing real issues in your life. That's all most folks need to know. That is the response to the query. However, if you're seeking a clear definition of what porn addiction is, certain symptoms of porn addiction, or the number of hours that constitutes an addiction, these answers don't exist.

The contentious application of an addiction paradigm to the usage of pornography is known as pornographic addiction. The use of pornography may contribute to compulsive sexual behavior, which can have detrimental effects on one's physical, mental, social, or financial health.

Behavioral addiction known as "porn addiction" is defined by an increasing need to watch pornographic media. In the past, someone with a pornography addiction would often watch or save pornographic movies, periodicals, and images to state their demand for the material. Thanks to the internet and other technology, the resources available to support a porn addiction have since developed, enabling anonymous access to endless pornography at all degrees of explicitness.

Pornography viewing has the potential to get obsessive and turn into an addiction. Pornography is more extensively utilized by college-age students and has gotten easier to

obtain. Up to 65% of young males and 18% of young women say they view pornography at least once each week.
People who get addicted to pornography more often and frequently go on to more intense content despite the repercussions. The inability to engage in sexual activity with a real person, self-harm, relationship issues, a negative influence on one's income or job, and adultery are only a few examples of negative effects.

The history of pornography

The history of pornography is practically hard to imagine since the term "pornography" itself is subjective. Images that may be seen as romantic or even holy in one civilization may be deemed obscene in another. Thus, 19th-century European visitors to India were horrified by what they saw as pornographic depictions of sexual interaction and intercourse in Hindu temples like those at Khajuraho (see photos); most contemporary viewers would likely have a different reaction. Similarly, many modern Muslim countries categorize several films and television shows that are acceptable in Western civilizations as "pornography." Pornography is very much in the eye of the beholder, to use a cliché.

In many ancient civilizations, explicit sexual behavior was often depicted in the framework of religion. For instance, phallic iconography and representations of orgiastic situations were common in ancient Greece and Rome, albeit it is unclear whether they had the same social or psychological purposes as contemporary pornography. In some of the most well-known sexual books, such as the Roman poet Ovid's Ars amatoria (Art of Love), a dissertation on the art of seduction, intrigue, and sensuous stimulation, a contemporary application appears more feasible. The Decameron, a collection of 100 tales by the Italian poet of the Middle Ages Giovanni Boccaccio, contains some licentious material. The depravity (and hypocrisy) of monks and other priests regarding sexual matters were a major motif in medieval pornography. Japan has a very advanced culture of visual erotica, although many of these works can't be called "pornographic" since they are so integrated into society. At least as early as the 17th century, there are elaborate representations of sexual activity—pictures ostensibly intended to teach sex instruction to medical practitioners, courtesans, and married couples. Makura-e (pillow images) was created to instruct and amuse married couples. The Tokugawa period (1603–1867) saw the peak of this fascination in highly frank erotica as new color woodblock printing technology made it simple to produce and distribute sensual prints, often known as shunga (literally, "pictures of spring"). By the 18th century, there was so much of this kind of literature that the government started issuing formal decrees banning it, which was followed by some arrests and trials. However, Japanese erotica persisted, and now, prints by masters like Suzuki Harunokbu (c. 1725–1770) are famous across the globe.

The Enlightenment (18th century), when printing technology had improved sufficiently to enable the creation of textual and visual materials to appeal to audiences of all socioeconomic levels and sexual preferences, marks the beginning of the modern era of Western pornography. A tiny black market for these publications in England served as the foundation for a distinct publishing and bookselling industry. The widely known Fanny Hill; or, Memoirs of a Woman of Pleasure (1748–49) by John Cleland is a classic from this period. Around this period, pornographic graphic art started to be made in large quantities in Paris and eventually became known in the English-speaking world as "French postcards."

Pornography developed as a potent tool for social and political protest in addition to its sexual component. It served as a platform for the investigation of radical concepts that were decried by both church and state, such as sexual freedom for all genders, the use of contraception, and abortion. Pornography was often used to expose the wrongdoings of royals and other nobles, which hurt the reputation of Europe's aristocracy. The Marquis de Sade was perhaps the most significant writer of socially radical pornography. His works, most notably Justine (1791), mixed orgiastic scenes with in-depth philosophical discussions on the ills of property and conventional social order.

By the time Queen Victoria assumed the throne in Great Britain in 1837, Holywell Street (also known as "Booksellers' Row") in London was home to more than 50 pornographic businesses. Despite—or maybe because of—the taboos on sexual subjects that were typical of the time, pornography thrived throughout the Victorian Era in Britain and the United States.

The development of photography and then motion pictures in the 19th century was soon used for the creation of pornography. Pornographic movies were publicly accessible as early as the 1920s, and their popularity skyrocketed in the

1960s. The advent of digital videodiscs (DVDs) in the 1990s and videocassettes in the 1980s made it possible to distribute pornographic movies widely and further promoted their usage since they could be seen in secret. With the introduction of the Internet in the 1990s, pornographic photos and movies were made much more accessible. One of the most lucrative industries on the Internet nowadays is the pornographic one. The Internet not only offered a sizable market for commercial pornography that catered to a wide range of tastes, but it also encouraged many amateurs to post pictures of themselves, often challenging conventional ideas of beauty and sex appeal. Webcam usage allowed people to publish live videos of themselves, often for a charge, further opening the market to amateurs. Child pornography is becoming more widely available because of the Internet.

In the idea that it depraves and corrupts both kids and adults and that it promotes the commission of sex crimes, pornography has long been denounced and legally outlawed. Occasionally, significant creative or even religious works have been outlawed due to these presumptions that they are pornographic. These presumptions have been refuted in the light of both legal and scientific evidence. Nevertheless, many nations have laws against obscenity that allow for the creation, dissemination, or ownership of pornographic items. A few decades ago, portrayals of sexual activity would have been seen as outrageously and criminally obscene, however, legal norms now vary greatly throughout Europe and North America. The prohibition of child pornography is the only taboo that is still largely upheld.

What Are the Signs of Porn Addiction?

According to studies, even a modest quantity of supernormal stimulation has the power to quickly modify the brain and behavior.

For instance, it only took 5 days to significantly increase healthy young individuals' sensitivities to video games. Although the gamers weren't dependent, their increased brain activity matched their irrational desire to play. In a different experiment, almost every rat was given unlimited access to "cafeteria food" and ate itself into obesity. After consuming junk food nonstop for a short time, the rats' dopamine receptors started to degenerate. As a result, they felt less satisfied after eating. The rats binged more as a result of feeling less satisfied.

Regarding Internet porn, this German research from the esteemed Max Planck Institute examined males who used the site sometimes. It discovered significant brain alterations linked to addiction. There was decreased functional connection between the intellectual and emotional areas of the brain as they watched more porn. The more porn they ingested, the less brain activity there was at the same moment. When someone becomes used to a specific level of stimuli, this is a typical symptom of desensitization. They eventually need more startling or peculiar content to be awakened.

According to Italian research, 16% of seniors in high school who watched pornography more than once per week had unusually low levels of sexual desire. In contrast, 0% of non-porn users claimed to have poor sexual arousal.

Regardless of ethnicity or economic level, compulsive sexual behaviors and pornography addiction afflict both men and women. And no one inside the church is safe. Why is porno so compelling? When a person encounters sexually suggestive visuals, their brain releases hormones that are naturally associated with pleasure. And when someone is feeling down, angry, lonely, weary, unwanted, rejected, or even simply uneasy, they could turn to sex and pornography to trigger this "pleasure system high," which can push them farther down the path to addiction to pornography.

Any use of pornography is wrong and prevents the abuser from having healthy perspectives on sex and relationships. Additionally, it gradually and quietly alters how the user views the other sex. This is since the brain develops resistance to the neurochemicals induced by the usage of pornography and needs new experiences to feel the same relaxation and pleasure. Therefore, regular use of pornography may lead to other sexual behaviors such as going to strip clubs, looking for prostitutes, having affairs, exhibitionism, voyeurism, sexual aggressiveness, or harassment. Pornography educates and tempts individuals to breach boundaries in ways that were previously unthinkable to them, even if not every user would follow such activities.

Do you suspect that you, your partner, or someone else you know has a pornography addiction? The five phases of pornography addiction are as follows:

1. Initial exposure.

As previously said, kids between the ages of twelve and seventeen are the biggest internet porn consumers. The majority of boys are curious about the other sex and, regrettably, believe they can find out more about them on websites that include pornography. They succumb to the allure of impersonal, emotionless touch. They are lured if they can't steer clear of this temptation. According to recent data, young guys are increasingly being diagnosed with erectile dysfunction as a result of abusing sophisticated pornography.

2. Dependence.

When the first naive curiosity about this degraded kind of sexual excitement develops into a physical reliance, addiction has occurred. Explicit sexual content serves as the habit-forming "substance" in pornography addiction. The addict utilizes the Internet, DVDs, his smartphone, periodicals, and books to feed his addiction.

Utilizing pornography becomes more than a harmless pastime. In the quest for the substance, the addict loses control of his or her mind. For visually-wired guys, the pictures stick in the brain and are difficult to forget. It is common practice to use porn to arouse oneself. The drug is absorbed through the eyes directly to the visual cortex at the back of the brain rather than a vein or lung, releasing neurochemicals like dopamine and endorphins to create a "high." The same brain modifications are seen in all addictions.

According to Gary Wilson of TEDx, "The Great Porn Experiment" can lead to addiction because of its constant novelty and ease of access. You get rewarded by dopamine for seeking out the visual pleasures that porn offers. You feel good after it. Some people are motivated to repeat this activity by brain chemicals. You return often. You cannot halt. You're addicted. Pornography addiction is seen as a kind of chemical brain damage as a result of this chemical release and the results of behavior. Pornography becomes a physical and emotional addiction for certain people.

3. Desensitization.

The quantity of pornography the addict previously consumed was insufficient to trigger these brain chemicals, just as with any pharmacological habit. Novelty appeals to dopamine. When the incentive wears off, the dopamine release decreases, causing pleasure and desire to fall as well as a possible male erectile dysfunction. Greater volumes of hardcore porn are desired when there is less immediate enjoyment. The vicious circle continues. Addicts must work harder to reactivate the pleasure centers in their brains to a higher degree.

4. Acceleration.

The addict increases the dosage because they want more excitement and novelty. They search the Internet for harmful, lewd photos. Their preferred medicine is now porn, and self-medication has reached new heights. Sexual fantasies, impulses, and pictures predominate in the mind. The overstimulation upsets the addict's brain's natural chemical equilibrium. They now have a strong need for novelty. Most watching takes place in private.

5. Sexual misbehavior.

The next phase of escalation is acting out. After seeing porn, the addict starts looking for real-world experiences. Risky behaviors result, including unexplainable anger, promiscuous sex, binge drinking to boost confidence to act out, and stealing from shared bank accounts to pay for prostitutes. In the latter, STDs may and do occur (Sexually Transmitted Diseases). Men and women who are hooked actively look for other live sex partners, leaving their dull husbands behind who have long since failed to satisfy their sexual needs. If they are married, the addict will not hesitate to commit adultery to satisfy their acute sexual novelty demand. Men will go to prostitutes, women will approach men in bars or the gym, or they will use online pornography (including email, chat rooms, and social media). Ask any spouse who has been the victim of their partner's porn addiction and has acted out in the cyber world: chatting with strangers who vicariously fulfill sexual cravings behind closed doors is adultery. It's emotional adultery and might cause behavior problems with real relationships.

Some addicts progress to deviant sexual activities and perversions including rape, child molestation, incest, and even murder depending on the amount of violent, hardcore porn the addict has seen to reach the acting out stage. One may think of porn as a starting point for more serious criminal activities.

THE TRUTH ABOUT PORNOGRAPHY— THE FALSEHOODS AND THE REALITY

Pornography has existed since prehistoric times. You may find drawings or carvings of individuals getting it on using a variety of techniques and materials if you look at some of the pictures discovered in caves and tombs. In India, Egypt, and a few locations in Europe, some of the earliest pictures have been discovered. Although they aren't as in-depth as the ones you see today, they are nevertheless instructive in their own right.

While some of the things you see in porn are believable, many of them are only for the enjoyment of many viewers and connoisseurs. In contrast to how most people are represented in reality, both male and female porn stars seem to be adaptable, open-minded, and double-jointed individuals. These porn stars themselves would never be caught doing the same things with their partners in real life that they do on camera. Making porn is merely a tool or a way to express one's creativity.

The truth is that, unless it is necessary for the production, what they do is not realistic in any way. These porn stars may not spend the same amount of time engaging in sexual activity as they would in real life. The scenes must be shot at particular angles, with the appropriate lighting, and with a specific set of sequences, just like in any other film. In actual

life, you would have to pause and take a break to do this. These gaps also make it difficult to have orgasms.
Aside from that, there are other characteristics of porn that are inappropriate for an intimate environment. Let's talk about a few of them and determine what is true and what is not.

1. "Pornography viewing just affects me and has no impact on others."
Similar to other addictions, there is a cascading effect from the behavior, and family members, friends, and other people suffer as a result of the addiction, sometimes with the addicted person being too engrossed in the addiction to recognize this. Young individuals who are pornographically addicted disregard crucial connections to feed their addiction.

2. "Pornography is an effective method of controlling sexual impulses without engaging in sexual activity."
Pornography constantly heightens sexual desire and cravings, as well as increases the likelihood of sexual acting out. The majority of individuals agree that young people engaging in sexual activity at an early age may have several detrimental effects.

3. "Pornography is a risk-free method to unwind and relax."
Pornography is extremely addicting and mentally corrosive, according to studies. The use of porn as a "relaxing" or stress-relieving activity hinders the development of healthy coping mechanisms for anxiety and stress. Young people, who should be learning healthy coping mechanisms to cope with stress, are especially harmed by this.

4. "Pornography is a useful tool for learning about sex."
In pornographic films, sexual scenes are often exaggerated and portrayed as incredibly thrilling and stimulating. These images frequently leave individuals who hope for comparable sensations dissatisfied since they provide an erroneous and unrealistic perspective of sexual encounters. Young individuals who compare their future wives to what they saw in pornographic photos may have an unrealistic perception of sexual encounters as a result of erroneous pornographic portrayals, which might prevent them from having a happy marriage.
Your future sexual experiences will become less intense if you watch porn, and the significance of sex in your future relationships will diminish. If young individuals who don't watch pornography haven't been hardened to it, their sexual connections with a future spouse will be more satisfying and meaningful.

5. "The persons represented in pornography are not presented as objects rather than as living beings."
Keep in mind that every individual you see is someone's daughter, sister, son, or brother. Would you want others to have a sexual interest in your future wife, spouse, daughter, sister, son, or brother?

6. "Pornography won't make me more sexually inclined."
You will have increased sexual cravings and thoughts after viewing porn. You will struggle to concentrate on the things in your life that are essential because you will get overwhelmed with thoughts of sexuality.

7. "Watching pornography has no moral consequences."
Viewing pornography affects your capacity and inclination to recognize right from wrong, making it simpler to excuse careless and dishonest actions. You could catch yourself rationalizing and lying to yourself about past absences from certain activities. When you're young, it's crucial to have a clear conscience since you'll be making choices that will affect the rest of your life.

8. "Pornography won't have an impact on my priorities in life."
Eventually, watching porn will take precedence over everything else in your life. Your pornography addiction will take precedence over the things in your life that ought to be your top priorities, such as your family, school, friends, extracurricular activities, and involvement in religious organizations.

9. "Pornography has no bearing on my relationship with God or my spirituality."
It is harder and harder to have a connection to God when watching porn. The brightness in your spirit will go, replaced with thoughts of gloom and pessimism. This is particularly crucial since fostering your spirituality as a young person can help you make many of the crucial choices that will affect your future.
10. "Watching pornography does not affect the way my brain is wired."
According to recent scientific studies, seeing pornography alters the structure of the brain in a way that is comparable to

how drugs alter the brain. Most young people are aware of the damaging consequences that drugs have on the brain, but far fewer are aware that pornographic viewing may have similar effects.

11. "Pornography may be watched as long as it is done in a manner that does not interfere with other activities of daily life."
Pornography is so compulsively appealing that you may find yourself losing hours in front of the TV or the Internet while also devoting a significant amount of time, effort, and money to feeding your addiction. You may be able to start by just watching sometimes, but over time you'll start to put off other things like schoolwork, time with family, and socializing in favor of watching porn.

12. "Once I find a committed relationship, I can stop looking at pornography."
Addictions are inherently tough to break, and doing so will affect how you interact with others in the future. Additionally, if you have a pornography addiction, you could pass up chances to acquire the personality traits that would enable you to participate in a fulfilling relationship, such as a happy marriage.

13. "Watching porn won't make me lose confidence."
The downward spiral of the addiction cycle causes a decline in happiness and life satisfaction while the addiction is maintained. When the exhilaration of watching pornography wears off, however, you are left feeling unhappy and

discouraged about carrying on with the practice even if you had intended to quit.

14. "Pornography lacks true addictive qualities. Simply resolve to give up searching.
While deciding to quit seeing is vital, many young people still view pornography despite their best efforts to stop. This is because addiction is so powerful. Young individuals who think they can simply decide to stop looking may be unaware of how powerful pornography's addictive nature is.

The Negative Effects of Porn

Do you believe that watching porn is just a fun and entertaining diversion? Think again. Since the advent of the internet, there has been tremendous growth in the quantity and diversity of porn, which has resulted in a dizzying array of social, interpersonal, and physical issues among porn consumers. Here are eight negative impacts that watching porn has on people:
The brain is genuinely altered by porn. Neurons, or brain cells, make up the brain and are triggered by a variety of inputs, including smell, sound, and sight. When stimulated, they produce substances that help the neurons' connections to one another to remain strong. Dopamine is a chemical that is produced when a person uses porn, and it is also released when a person uses an addictive drug. When exposed to porn often, the brain becomes overloaded with dopamine. To deal with the overload, the brain eliminates certain dopamine receptors, which therefore makes it harder for the porn user to experience the effects as strongly as he did previously. As a

result, the brain is trained to need increasing amounts of dopamine to experience the early effects. When someone uses porn often, the amount of dopamine needed to experience thrill is so elevated that they can no longer solely enjoy the things that used to make them joyful.

Effects of Pornography That Are Bad

Despite prior emotional relationships—whether between the mother and father or between the parents and the child—pornography is strong enough to overwhelm individuals, couples, and families. Adults, kids, couples, families, and society all suffer from pornography. Pornography inhibits healthy sexual development in teenagers, and it alters sexual views and social norms in adults. The use of pornography in families causes marital unhappiness, infidelity, separation, and divorce. Pornography still has an impact on society as a whole. For instance, child sex offenders often take part in both the watching and the sharing of porn. The harmful impacts of pornography on our own lives, children, families, and society at large are listed here.

1. Family Effects of Pornography Viewing

Throughout all phases of family life, pornography has a tremendous impact. A youngster who is exposed to porn in a familial environment experiences stress and is more likely to have unfavorable ideas about the nature and function of human sexuality. When teenagers watch pornography, they develop new perspectives on their own and other people's sexuality, which shapes their sexual expectations and conduct. Pornography has negative, even disastrous, impacts on marriage for adults.

2. Desensitization, boredom, and habit

In addition to producing habituation, boredom, and sexual unhappiness in viewers, prolonged exposure to pornography is linked to more tolerant attitudes toward extramarital sex and recreational attitudes toward sex. Research of first-year college students revealed that regular porn viewing increased their tolerance for sexually explicit content, necessitating the usage of more innovative and odd material to elicit the same degree of arousal or interest. For instance, the habit may cause someone to engage in anal intercourse, watch "depictions of group sex, sadomasochistic activities, and sexual interaction with animals," and trivialize "nonviolent forms of the sexual abuse of minors."

Men who watch a lot of porn may find their partners to be less seductive, which will decrease their pleasure with their affection, attractiveness, and sexual prowess. Pornography may increase the urge for more intense sexual stimulation, which can make people feel bored in traditional relationships and more likely to look for sex outside of marriage. A viewer's perception of "recreational sexual encounters" alters with repeated exposure to pornography, and they become far more receptive to sexual permissiveness.

3. A distorted view of reality

Sexual access is portrayed in pornography as unrelenting, "a sporting event that amounts to innocent fun," with minimal effects on feelings, perceptions, and health. But this is not the case. Pornography causes distorted perceptions of social reality, including an exaggerated perception of the level of sexual activity in the general population, an increased assessment of male and female promiscuity, "an overestimation of almost all sexual activities performed by sexually active adults," and an exaggerated perception of the prevalence of perversions like group sex and bestial behavior in general. Therefore, the perceptions that a pornographic spectator has are quite different from reality. These misunderstandings lead to the adoption of three ideas: (1) that sexual encounters are just recreational; (2) that males are typically sexually motivated; and (3) that women are mere commodities or sex objects.

4. Objectification and Feminist Disrespect for Women
Pornography encourages the notion that it is OK to degrade women. Exposure to sexual and even semi-sexual content via the Internet, periodicals, and television are linked to increased beliefs that women are sex objects or sexual commodities because men use pornography significantly more often than women. Men who have been exposed in this way are more inclined to refer to women in openly sexual terms than by other characteristics.

5. Unwanted pregnancies and sexually transmitted diseases
Users of pornography are more likely to develop a sexually transmitted disease or father an unplanned pregnancy because pornography promotes sexually permissive attitudes and behavior. The 87 percent of the time that sexual activity is depicted in pornography without the use of condoms is a call to the promiscuous to get an STD, have an unmarried child, and have multiple sex partners. Additionally, pornography

encourages sexual compulsivity, which increases a person's risk of contracting an STD twofold.

6. Sexual Dependence

Pornography and "cybersex" may result in sexually compulsive behaviors that impair a person's ability to accomplish other important life activities. They are also extremely addictive. In one research, more than 90% of the therapists polled thought that someone may get addicted to "cybersex." In a US poll, 57% of regular viewers admitted to using internet sex as a stress reliever. According to a 2006 Swedish survey of habitual Internet pornographers, 6% of them were obsessive users, who also consumed much more non-Internet porn. The use of addictive pornography lowers self-esteem and impairs one's capacity to have a fulfilling social and professional life. They loathed the "out of control" sensation and the time commitment that their pornography usage created, according to a poll of pornography addicts.

7. Aggression and Mistreatment

Intense usage of pornography is highly associated with sexual violence, and among porn fans, there is a noticeable rise in sexual callousness, including the aforementioned "rape myth acceptance." Pornography often contains violent material. According to a survey of various pornographic media, violence was present in over 42% of internet pornography, over 25% of video sequences, and nearly 25% of magazine scenes. According to the second research, non-consensual sex was present in over half of violent Internet situations. However, males who watch violent pornography (i.e., shows of rape or torture) are more likely to engage in sexual violence. The statistics indicate "a small link between exposure to pornography and future behavioral aggressiveness." Pornography negatively affects schizophrenic guys, who are more prone to act on their urges, which is dangerous.

8. Effect on Kids

The effects of parental pornography consumption on young children are complex and upsetting. The warmth of a loving family life, which is a child's natural social nourishment, is eliminated by pornography. The exposure to pornographic material that a parent has obtained as well as the higher likelihood of the kids becoming pornography consumers is some additional losses and traumas associated with the usage of pornography while a child is young.

9. The effect on teenagers

Teenagers who watch porn are disoriented at that stage of development when they must learn how to manage their libido and when they are most susceptible to ambiguity about their moral and sexual convictions. Sexually explicit Internet content substantially raised the sexuality-related doubts of 2,343 teenagers, according to research. The research also revealed a decline in marital commitment to the other spouse and an increase in views favoring sexual experimentation with individuals outside of marriage as a result of increasing exposure to sexually explicit Internet content. Frequent pornography usage is also significantly associated with feelings of loneliness, and even severe depression.

High teenage pornography usage has an impact on behavior as well. The use of male pornography is associated with much more non-romantic friend sex and is probably related to the so-called "hook-up" culture.

10. A Rise in Infidelity.
One research of teenagers demonstrates that regular pornographic usage typically results in the abandoning of loyalty to girlfriends. Another research discovered a significant link between using the internet to watch pornography and engaging in sexually permissive conduct. According to Stack's research, persons who use prostitution for sexual purposes consume Internet pornography 3.7 times more often than those who do not.

Porn ruined these people's lives

Do murderers or serial killers have any traits? I think they do base on the hundreds of crime dramas I've seen.
Now, I'm no expert, but I thought it could be interesting to check whether convicted murderers and serial killers ever admitted to having a pornographic interest. I did this since blocking Internet porn is one of Net Nanny's objectives, and our business places a high priority on preventing addiction to pornography.
Although watching violent pornography doesn't always lead to violent conduct, I think that it may make aggressive or violent inclinations worse if a person already has them by making them feel like their dreams are "normal."
The information on many convicted serial murderers from the past is compiled in the paragraphs that follow.

· Wisconsin serial murderer Jeffrey Dahmer described his pre-victim search process as consisting of "just...using photographs of former victims...the pornographic movies, the mags." 17 boys and men were slain by Jeffrey Dahmer.

· Ted Bundy, a Washington resident who was convicted of rape and mutilation murder, said that hard-core pornography had a "crystallizing impact" on his violent impulses and outbursts in the 1970s.

· Utah's Arthur Gary Bishop, who was killed for raping and killing five boys in the 1980s, said that pornography had a "devastating" impact on him.
· At least 53 women and children were killed by the Russian serial murderer Andrei Chikatilo."...with photographs of nude women in his cell, he attributed his problems to pornography."

· In the 1950s, Wisconsin resident Ed Gein—the first serial murderer and inspiration for the films Psycho, Maniac, and The Silence of the Lambs—amassed a collection of anatomy books, porn magazines, horror, and adventure literature.

· John Wayne Gacy's wife filed for divorce in 1976 citing her husband's "erratic moods" and the discovery of his collection of children-focused pornographic magazines. In Chicago, Illinois, Gacy murdered at least 33 young men and boys.

· BTK (bind, torture, kill) was the moniker given to Kansas native Dennis Rader, who murdered 10 people." He maintained thorough notes of his fantasies and crimes in his collection of pornography, which he referred to as the "mother lode."

· In New York, David Berkowitz murdered nearly a dozen individuals. When he joined a cult, "drug usage, sadistic pornography, and violent criminality" were introduced to him. Additionally, the group produced and disseminated child pornography.

· Richard Ramirez was shown graphic images of his cousin "raping Vietnamese women and cutting off the skulls of Vietcong troops." In California, he murdered at least 13 people in return.

· Edmund Kemper, a notorious necrophile and serial murderer from California known as the Co-ed Killer, picked up hitchhiking women, murdered them, and raped them after their deaths using pornography and detective magazines as sensual stimuli.

· Florida resident Ottis Toole developed an obsession with homosexual porn. At the age of 14, he "committed his first murder." He murdered 108 people while on his murderous rampage, and Henry Lee Lucas was at his side.

· Lonnie Franklin Jr., a.k.a. The Grim Sleeper, "had a fondness for prostitutes and pornography." He was a resident of Los Angeles and would pick up prostitutes, photograph them in porn, and then strangle them to death. He killed 11 people throughout his murderous spree.

· The judge told killer Stuart Hazell in the 2013 case of 12-year-old UK child Tia Sharp that the data of his mobile phone's internet searches "made abundantly apparent that you were seeking out pornographic photos of pre-teen females."

The use of pornography probably won't lead the casual viewer to commit violent acts; in the cases cited above, their behaviors included pornography use. In 2013, on the day that Mark Bridger, a UK native, kidnapped April Jones, he "viewed online photographs of a young girl and a pornographic cartoon depicting...rape." Pornography, in my opinion, has substantial and long-lasting effects on conduct.

Porn is ruining your sense of manhood.

A man's inherent urge and desire to seek out the other sex will be indefinitely suppressed by constant exposure to pornography.

Both masturbation and pornographic viewing are fatal for a guy. You feel guilty, ashamed, and lethargic after masturbating. Your mind will be programmed to believe that women should only be regarded in a sexual context if you are constantly exposed to pornographic content. Additionally, it will hinder your success in interacting with women in real life.

It's simple for males to sit at home and stoke their sexual cravings thanks to pornography. We did not develop in this way.

What porn fails to tell us is that the farther a user enters that dream world, the more probable it is that their reality will turn out to be the complete opposite.
Researchers discovered that after seeing softcore porn, both men and women were much less satisfied with their partner's attractiveness, willingness to attempt new sex acts, and sexual performance. This was shown in one of the largest studies on porn consumption ever undertaken.
By training their brains to get aroused by sitting alone in front of a computer rather than being with a real person, porn users destroy their capacity to perform sexually in real life.
A fully mature individual must have sexual self-control at some time in their life. Your sexual urge should not be your master; rather, you should learn to manage and regulate it.
In addition, watching many hours of porn leads to preconceived notions about what sex is like. The typical 16-year-old who views porn is learning about sex from the movies he or she sees. And that's bad, particularly considering that porn promotes a distorted dream and a blown-up reality of what actual sex is like.
We are aware that one of the main ingredients in luring ladies is self-confidence. Masturbation and porn viewing seriously undermine one's sense of value and self-esteem.
The capacity to establish, accomplish and appreciate significant objectives may be destroyed by porn. Any fleeting pleasure is not worth that.
Fundamentally, it is a vicious loop that prevents males from summoning the guts to approach women, much alone captivate and seduce them.

Social anxiety and porn.

It's never been simpler to spend an increasing amount of time online nowadays. In addition to being a potent tool, the internet can also be a potent temptation, particularly when it comes to pornography.

While porn has many diverse psychological impacts, most individuals are unaware that social anxiety is one of them. Today, we'll examine the numerous ways that a porn addiction may alter your brain and increase your susceptibility to stressful situations.

Social anxiety: What is it?

We must first comprehend what this impact is to discover how porn activates it in the brain. Feelings of inadequacy and the worry that others will evaluate you harshly are the two characteristics that constitute social anxiety. Any social engagement, even ones that first appear unimportant, might set off these feelings.

As you may expect, having a serious influence on social anxiety is having a porn (or internet) addiction. In rare circumstances, it could even cause an issue that wasn't there before. Let's examine the cause of this.

Self-esteem and porn

Most of the time, one's self-esteem might be connected to social anxiety. You are far more inclined to presume that other people see you the same way if you don't respect yourself highly. Unfortunately, even if your self-esteem was initially robust, porn may significantly reduce it.

Many people claim to have diminished sentiments of worth after viewing porn. However, why is that so? Typically, there are a few explanations for this.

First off, the characters in pornographic films are often quite gorgeous and enticing. You may feel inadequate to live up to their expectations while comparing yourself to them.
The size of the penis might enhance this impact in males. Watching porn might exacerbate the feelings of inadequacy that many guys already have over their size. The males in pornographic content are often above average, which might give all men the impression that they aren't competitive.
The second way that porn might undermine one's self-worth is by drawing attention to one's sexual prowess. For instance, if you're single and a porn addict, this might exacerbate how lonely you feel. You feel that you're missing out or can't have the same experiences since you're not partaking in the same sexual acts as those folks on TV.
Finally, porn may influence one's desire and sexual performance. In many circumstances, seeing too much graphic material might make you less effective in the bedroom, which can damage your self-esteem. Regardless of their pornographic preferences, men might have performance anxiety, but an addiction to the medium can significantly worsen symptoms.
Overall, the impacts of porn and how it affects your self-esteem might make you more socially anxious. You start to worry more and more about being evaluated by others, even those who are close to you, as your self-esteem declines. The consequences might worsen with time and cause social disengagement.

Addiction to porn and shame

While viewing sexual material on its own might lower your self-esteem, concealing your behaviors out of shame can exacerbate issues like social anxiety. It might be very difficult to establish strong social relationships if you're always concerned that your significant other, friends, or family will learn about your addiction.

Your shame may grow along with your addiction as it gets more pervasive, to the point where you want to avoid all social situations to protect yourself from the weight of being discovered. In severe circumstances, it may take the form of social isolation, which may lead to a wide range of additional issues.

Internet and Social Anxiety

While watching porn may have a significant negative influence on your brain and sense of self, spending too much time online generally can have a similar effect. As a result, if you continue to spend too much time online and get hooked on sexual information, your social anxiety may become worse much more quickly.

Why does excessive internet use cause these issues? Here are some of them.

• Social Insulation: When you're online, you may protect yourself by remaining in a certain social "bubble" of others. You avoid leaving that bubble at all costs since doing so might make you anxious.

• Lack of Interaction - Spending more time online means less time interacting with others. Your anxiety levels may rise as you start to overthink and overanalyze everything if you aren't exposed to social interactions.

Reverse the Cycle

You must start down the road to recovery if you don't want to become paralyzed by social anxiety (or any of the other many side effects brought on by a porn addiction). Fortunately, if you have a network of people who can assist you, doing this can solve both issues at once.

Your addiction does not have to define who you are. The first step towards solving a problem is admitting that you have one.

WILLPOWER IS NOT ENOUGH

Someone battling with a pornography addiction is one of the most frequent things we hear in counseling. Both men and women struggle with this temptation daily, and they both often give in to it when they are weak. They don't get why they can't easily refrain from gazing at it or giving in to temptation. They leave their laptops, phones, and tablets unrestrained and rely on their power of will to keep themselves away from the exact sin that is killing them, much like a serial dieter who maintains a buffet of cupcakes, cookies, and sweets in the pantry.

That isn't how resisting temptation works.

Willpower by itself is insufficient. Like everything else in the human body, willpower may wear out. You won't have to strain yourself as much if you use the above-ground fencing and the trails underneath. The majority of our actions are unconscious. This only involves developing methods for using our unconscious to our advantage.

Installing filters and accountability software on every gadget in your house is a must if you are battling a porn addiction and are determined to quit viewing porn. I'll demonstrate how to restrict access to sexual and other pornographic material on Android smartphones. Alcoholics must empty their bottles, dieters must discard their cupcakes, and porn addicts must block porn. This is the way to resist temptation.

When a significant pleasure is taken away, a vacuum results that must be filled. If you don't replace the hole with healthy pleasures, ultimately it will be filled with something that isn't healthy for you. If pleasure is temporarily withheld, the vacuum will close, but why make things more difficult for yourself? I refer to the practice of using many little joys to make life easier while I adjust to not having one significant pleasure from the past as "pleasure stacking." Additionally, it lessens the likelihood of beginning a new addiction during that period. Here are my recommended routes:

• Mindfulness meditation: I was able to make the strongest connection between my abstinence and my practice of mindfulness meditation. Numerous benefits of meditation (scientifically proven). It enhances mental focus and self-control. You'll find it easier to shift your attention when a daydream appears in your thoughts by letting it go. decreases stress and other unpleasant emotions dramatically. More importantly, it helps you become more conscious of what those bad emotions are so that you don't let them control you. The mind is so calm and pure after meditation that it feels fantastic.

• Exercise - after a few days, you'll inevitably discover that you have a certain level of energy that has to be expended in some way. We lose our minds if we don't use our energy, much like a dog that isn't taken for walks. When I don't PMO, exercising is a lot simpler, and it's a very beneficial method to feel good (after a workout), reduce stress, enhance sleep (remember how crucial it is to go to sleep fast when coming into bed), and feel good in general.

• Socialize - Although I sometimes still have anxiety when I'm with others, I often feel better than ever when I wake up the next morning. Social needs are unquestionably connected to this since it has to do with the hormone of love and connection known as oxytocin, a brain transmitter.

• Get a snuggle partner for the same reasons as previously. I have this lady that comes over, and we often just lie around watching TV. It's nice because it's a great way to connect and open up. My heart is warmed by it. The seemingly insignificant act of just relaxing next to someone and being silent may have great results over the coming days.

• A gratitude journal is available under solo tools on the YBOP website. Excellent data demonstrates that doing this little item consistently will boost your mood in general.

• Having SMART objectives. These are SMART (specific, measurable, achievable, realistic, and time-bound) objectives. It's not realistic to declare, "I'm never going to look at a female again." I dislike the 90-day challenge because it places the objective at a point when it becomes problematic. I know that placing a 90-day chart on my wall made the objective seem tough and undermined my self-belief. Instead, I should merely concentrate on brief periods at a time, such as the weekend and then the week. Having been through this myself, I now take things one day at a time and concentrate exclusively on what may assist or hinder me in the present (while knowing in the back of my mind that this behavioral change is for life).

• Establish a bedtime routine that will help you fall asleep as quickly as possible once you are in bed and get the best night's sleep possible so that when you wake up, you are refreshed and can get out of bed more easily. This is especially important if your vulnerable situations involve being in bed. Our mood and ability to handle stress depend on getting a good night's sleep. One thing that is essential for me is to turn off all devices, including my phone, around ten minutes before going to bed and about twenty minutes before. This makes me tired. If I have a bedtime ritual, I always feel rejuvenated when I wake up.

• Self-hypnosis: If you're still one of those individuals who think hypnosis is a kind of mind control or sorcery, I advise you to do further study. Amazingly, hypnosis may assist with a variety of objectives. Unfortunately, from the standpoint of a hypnotherapist, the majority of iTunes audio downloads, particularly for erotica, aren't really great (but they do help, especially if you listen frequently). Additionally, you may utilize the audio files to address other PMO-related concerns including stress, sleep, exercise & motivation, etc. You may also pay a little bit extra to visit a hypnotherapist in person, however. It's ironic that at the time when I was a student of hypnosis, I resisted getting professional assistance at all costs, but once I did, things became a million times simpler.

- Eliminate temptations: This may include eliminating or restricting your use of social media and other sources of temptations using the technique I'll explain in the following chapter.

TRIGGERS & HOW TO AVOID THEM

What is a trigger?

Each "expert" approaches them in a unique way. Since "trigger" is a conceptual term, everyone will have a different viewpoint. Of course, it has now been appropriated by contemporary social media meme-speak. #Triggered

"Something that precipitates a certain occurrence or scenario" is the term from the dictionary that applies the most. It implies "to hurry the occurrence of" when you precipitate. So, if we're trying to come up with a clear explanation for someone who struggles with porn, a trigger is anything that makes me turn to porn. That definition seems reasonable to me, but it needs to be broken down and clarified a little. It's crucial to realize that a trigger is not a temptation. In fact, if you recall nothing else from this, keep it in mind.

We come with triggers in a variety of positive and bad spheres of our existence. When I eat one of my Gramma's Christmas cookies, the taste and look take me back to being at her home when she was baking.

Consider a trigger as the first item that makes you think about pornography.

Recognize your own triggers.

Environmental or emotional/mental triggers are also possible.

To put it another way, triggers might be internal (caused by anything that arises in my heart, soul, body, or mind) or external (something said, seen, or done). You should think about both kinds as you strive to determine your own. We often overlook the external ones in favor of the "internal" ones, which is the emphasis of models for recovering from addiction like H.A.L.T.

When triggers are discussed, they are often meant to refer to those internal triggers. The H.A.L.T. model of cognition proposes that if you see yourself being drawn into negative thoughts or behaviors (self-harm, drinking, etc.), you should first determine if you are physically or metaphorically hungry, angry, lonely, or weary. If you satisfy that need, the urge to engage in harmful conduct will go.

While this specific strategy didn't help me break away from pornography, it still helps me fight my guilt and bad thoughts. If I feel myself sinking into a hole of misery, one of these four reasons is generally to blame.

You probably have an internal trigger if you often find yourself fleeing towards the calm, dark, and anonymity of porn.

It doesn't necessarily have to fit into the H.A.L.T. categories, in my experience. When I was ill or under stress, I would often turn to porn, but I would also turn to it to "treat myself" when I was joyful.

Asking yourself whether pornography (or desire, imagination, or masturbation) seems like an escape may help you identify your own triggers for emotions and mental states.

If the response is affirmative, then consider "from what." If you're having trouble utilizing the term "escape," consider if you could be using porn as a "numbing agent." If the answer is affirmative, you must next consider what it is that you are attempting to numb. The most of the time, you'll need to repair that area before you can battle effectively.

Determine your environmental triggers.

When we speak of liberation and rehabilitation, we frequently forget to include this. I believe that we get too focused on the internal work, particularly as Christians. But keep in mind that triggers are not alluring. Here, the church's "heart work" must learn to get along with the biological truths of who we are as people.

External cues activate our physical brains, while interior impulses activate our metaphorical hearts. If you've ever encountered, battled, or depended on pornography (or desire, fantasy, or masturbation), those experiences become memories, and those memories are just as real.

Not all triggers need to be negative.

If the trigger is severe in and of itself, you may even need to go back a few steps on your road since you could be mistaking it for your first fall. Say, "Well, erotica is a trigger for me," for example. That is untrue. The first step in falling is erotica. You need to go back and assess what caused you to first get interested in erotica.

Triggers may not be obvious.

For example, I discovered that a large bottle of lotion I owned was a trigger when I was attempting to overcome my addiction. I had purchased it before to leaving for college, thinking that the full 32 ounces would be plenty to last me the entire four years. I used it exclusively throughout my first year of college. That was also the height of my porn addiction, thus someway in my mind, the scent of my mango cocoa butter body lotion became mixed up with porn. Every time I used it, I noticed a strange desire for porn. As ludicrous as it appeared, I made the link and tossed the lotion away.

You may have no control over triggers.

Since we have a lot of control over our surroundings, dealing with external stimuli is simpler. However, sometimes there isn't much we can do to prevent or alter a trigger. For instance, many of us women have triggers at various times throughout our menstrual cycle. There isn't much we can do to alter that—basically nothing. Keep in mind that triggers are not sin or temptation. These are the things that first make you think of pornography (or lust, fantasy, or masturbation). Even if you can't control the trigger itself, you can always control the decisions that link "trigger" to "action" since you still have to make them in reaction to the triggers.

TWO SUPER EFFECTIVE ANDROID APPS TO BLOCK PORN (HOW TO SET THEM UP)

We already know that although willpower can only go so far in preventing us from engaging in porn, since it is so accessible, we will inevitably give in at some time. On Twitter, browsers, erotic Telegram sites, twerk videos on Instagram, and even Facebook, it will be here in only 10 seconds.

Our weakest times, when we are most likely to be alone and bored, are the times when we need to prevent access to such programs the most. If we really want to eradicate this illness, we must be prepared to make some unpopular decisions or the illness will devour us.

There are 2 key applications on Google Play that will aid us in winning this conflict:

1. **Spin Safe Browser**

You and your children may use Spin Safe Browser to surf the internet without running across any upsetting Images or Videos. On your Android smartphones and tablets, SPIN Safe Browser is a web browser with built-in web filtering that's intended to protect you from unsuitable material. Pornography, nudity, and other offensive material are all immediately prohibited. This protects you and your kids from potentially harmful information.

Install Spin Safe Browser and disable all other mobile browsers.

2. Applock Fingerprint-based

Disabling any function on your smartphone that permits app termination without accessing the phone's primary settings is the first step in this process. This is the biggest threat we face. With simply one click, applications may be terminated. To identify this function and deactivate it, we must search through your phone.

Then, as seen below, open the Google Playstore app and search for "Applock - Fingerprint." Install the app.

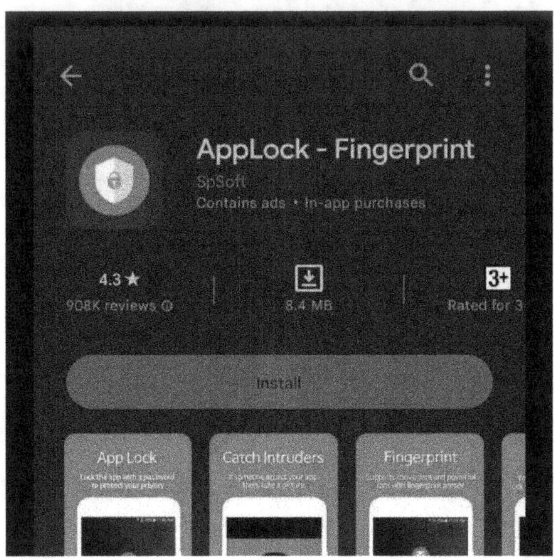

The "Device Administrator" option may be found in your phone's settings. After installation, turn it on for Applock - Fingerprint. This function is available on all Android phones. Yours may be located in the "security" section of your phone's settings. This will stop the app from being uninstalled when it is supposed to be locked.

Open the installed app and choose a four-digit password to sign up for the service.

Make sure not to select “YES” to the next phase that pops up. It has to be “NO”, else you risk unlocking the app freely with your fingerprint.

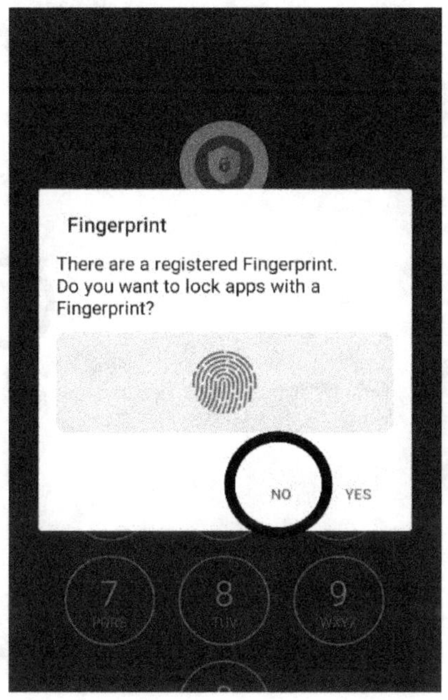

Choose the applications that will allow you to view erotica or pornographic material. I've chosen Twitter, Telegram, and even the file-sharing program Xender in the picture below. It's not safe for me to use the app since it gives you access to your social media accounts. To choose the programs you wish to prohibit, tap the button with a black circle around it. To add each of the apps you've chosen, tap the plus symbol.

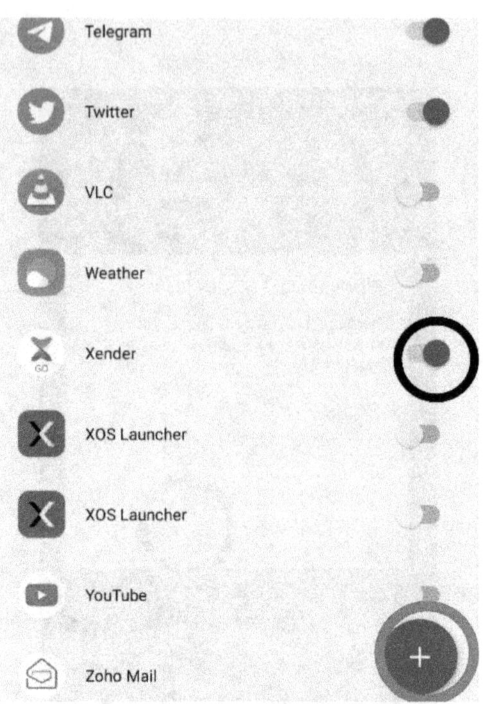

NOTE: You must select settings and package installer among apps to be blocked.

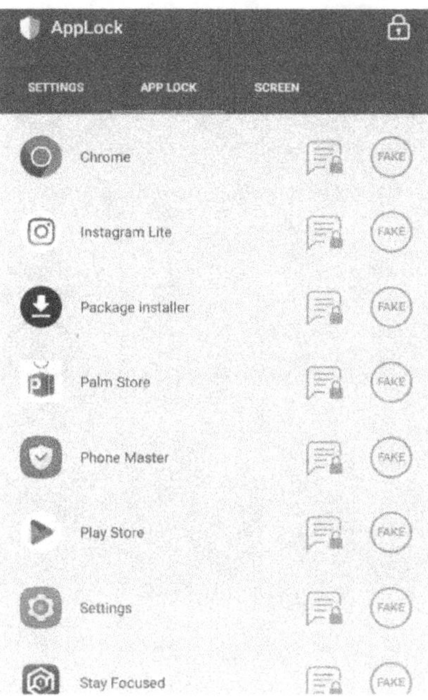

After selecting the apps, you follow the prompts that will pop up on your screen to allow access to notification, allow accessibility and display over other applications feature.

Now go to "settings" at the top left corner and tap ON the settings circled below

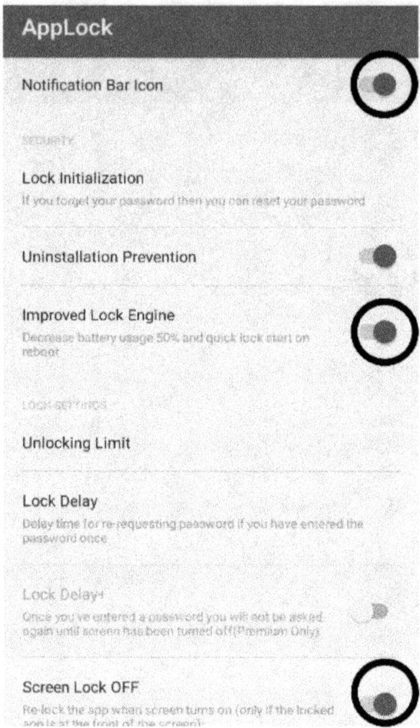

Install Helper.

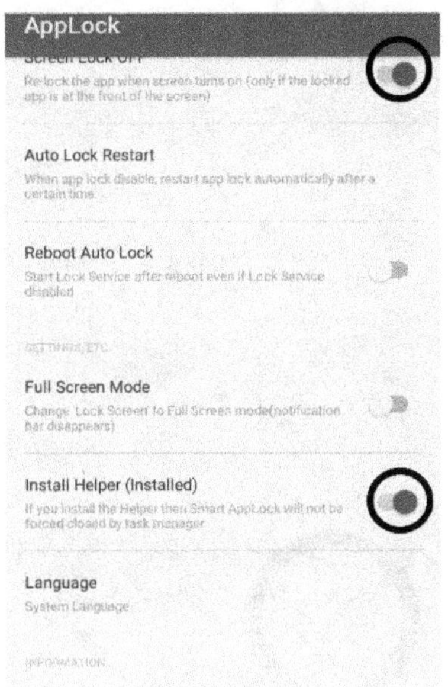

After setting up, tap on “Smart lock”

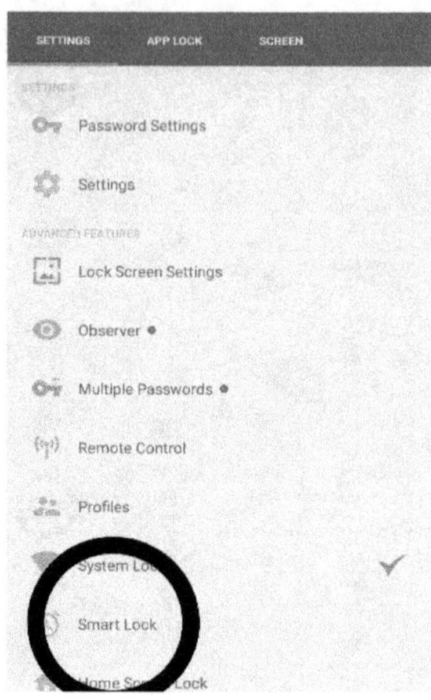

Tap on the 3 dots by the top right corner and tap on "Older version"

Tap on "App Lock Time" to turn it on. Then tap on "Time Set"

I would suggest setting the "Lock Time (Daily)" at a time when you are certain to be at home if you live alone. For instance, if you are certain to return home before 19:00 pm and leave for work before 8:00 am. In such situation, your most susceptible hours are from 20:00 pm to 7:00 am. The lock will be set between (20:00pm and 7:30am).

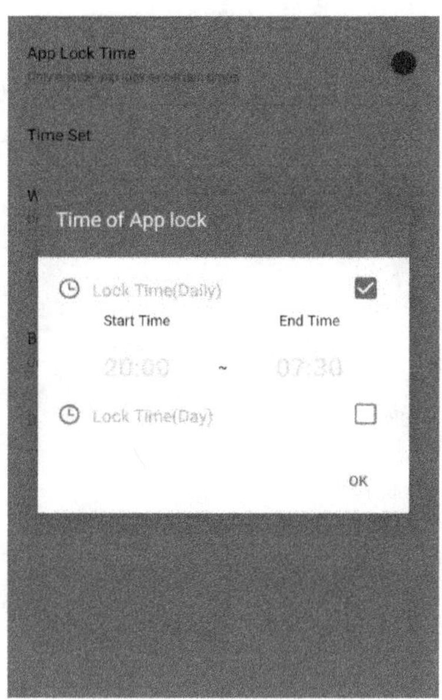

The disadvantage of using the "Lock Time (Daily)" feature is that you'll have access to pornography during the daytime during the weekend since your lock period is usually set for nights only.

The solution to that is the "Lock Time (Day)" feature. You can set the lock period for each day of the week starting from 00:00 am till any time within the day when you won't be vulnerable. See the image below for an example of how to block the apps on weekdays and weekends.

If you live with a friend or your family, then you can still give yourself some liberty knowing you can't view porn while they are around you. The tricky time comes when your friend or family member is asleep. If they tend to sleep most time at

00:00 am, then your lock needs to start around this time. You can set your "Lock Time (Daily)" between (00:00 am and 7:30 am).

Lock Time(Daily) ☐

Lock Time(Day) ☑

	Start Time		End Time
Mon	00:00	~	07:30
Tue	00:00	~	07:30
Wed	00:00	~	07:30
Thu	00:00	~	07:30
Fri	00:00	~	07:30
Sat	00:00	~	20:00
Sun	00:00	~	20:00

The image above shows that I'm vulnerable during the weekend between 00:00 and 20:00 when I'm home alone, so I have set my lock time between this period. You can play around the time to see what timeframe works best for you.

Additionally, if you are usually at home—perhaps because you work from home—I advise locking those triggering applications for the whole time you are certain to be at home.

If the cleaning button terminates the Applock app, you may also activate the lock for the "Recent Apps (Multitasking)" option under "system lock" in the settings section.

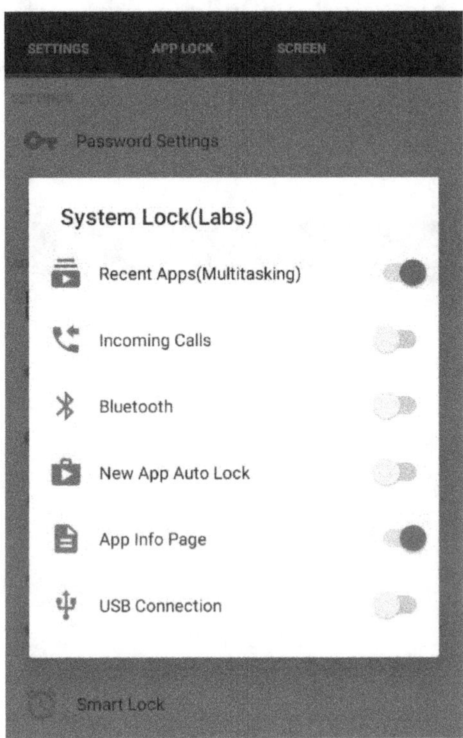

Password Change

This step should only be done when you are sure that you have set every other aspect of the app correctly because you might not be able to enter the app again after the password is changed.

Remember you used a four-digit password when you opened the application, you have to change that password to one that even you won't remember.

Go to your notepad on your device and type out random characters (like this - wjdiwe9u3rnejfubfoejf) and copy/cut it. That will be your new password. Do not save that password anywhere for future use.

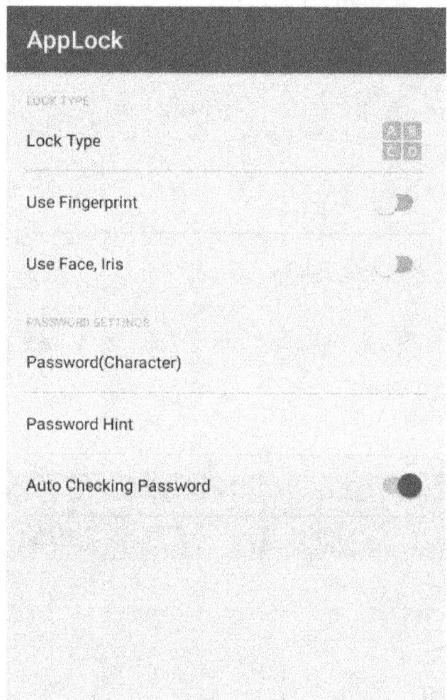

Go to "Password settings" under Settings

Tap on "Lock Type" and change it to "Password (Character)." Now you have to register the new password. Paste the new password twice and it will be saved as the new password.

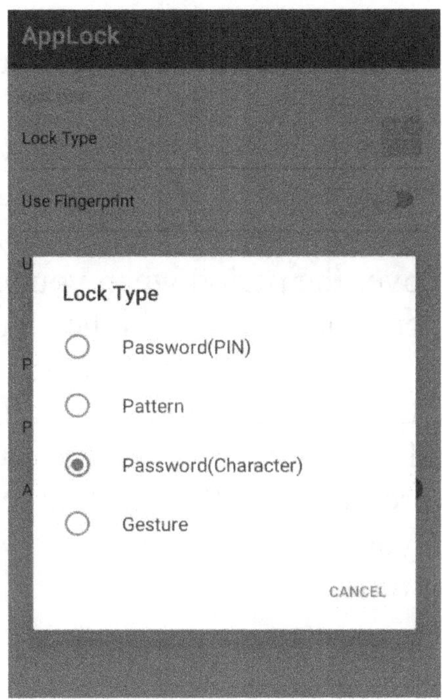

This is to prevent you from unlocking any app when you are filled with the urge to watch porn.

This is a tough decision that one has to make the recovery process easier. This minor discomfort is definitely for the greater good of ourselves, our immediate and future family, and the entire society. We must not let this evil destroy the life we have been given.

What if I still relapse?

Sometimes we may underestimate the amount of time we will be alone. One of the aforementioned causes may result in a relapse.

To make sure that it doesn't happen again, you would need to implement strict procedures.

You may sometimes need to adjust the time window in which your Appblock is operational to account for unanticipated events. You should remove the program, reinstall it, and then set it up again to cover the period when you are most exposed if there will be a permanent change in the alone time. Additionally, you may download any time-based lock software from the Google Play Store, including "Stay Focused." This adds another barrier to the usage of pornography and provides you the freedom to lock applications when you know you'll be alone yourself for an unexpectedly long time.

Many of us have computers as well, which nevertheless allow us to browse porn. I'll suggest that you look for software that will prevent you from accessing porn. I've used K9 web protection software for laptops before, and it's entirely free and does its job to a very high degree. The catch here is that if you register for the program using your email address, you won't be able to change your password at any time.

Another thing that helps me avoid thinking about porn while using my phone or laptop is gospel music. Connecting with greater power—in my case, God's power—has a certain allure. It diverts your attention from worldly concerns and focuses it on idealistic ideas. You may attempt this as well as establish a connection with a higher power that you believe in. As soon as you turn on your gadget, play gospel music and listen to the words. Let the song speak to your addiction and you, and I'm certain that God will direct your heart.

HOW TO HANDLE A RELAPSE

For many people in recovery from sex addiction, quitting online pornography permanently is almost difficult. Internet pornography differs from other forms of sexual expression in that it grabs people's attention quickly and may have a strong grip that causes recurrent relapses even after other, more harmful activities have been abandoned.

If you are dependent on serial affairs or sexual massage parlors, you need at the very least make a very basic strategy. This enables the use of mindfulness techniques and other tools to aid in stopping the behavior.

There is sexual imagery everywhere, and it may sometimes appear unexpectedly on computer screens. My coworker had a relapse after seeing a friend's hot Valentine's Day video on Facebook. Getting rid of your PCs is not the best long-term option, and blocking software is unreliable.

The main causes of relapse in chronic online pornography

Similar to other addictions, porn addiction has similar root causes. Internet porn addicts, like other sex addicts, tend to be emotionally isolated, equate closeness with pain, and avoid interacting with others.

However, I think there are several very important risk factors for porn addiction that often go untreated and neglected, even when using conventional treatment techniques. Which are:

• Giving up on a genuine and long-lasting emotional and sexual connection; • Leading a simple life; • Getting into a regular pattern that encourages porn usage
New Behaviors Are Required for Relapse Prevention
You may still need to make some very significant adjustments to your life after overcoming a sex addiction to resist the allure of porn.

Make life-filled plans.
Make a longer-term strategy for how you're going to transform your life into one of success and purpose if you now live in deprivation, are prepared to live in untidy conditions or are willing to be an underachiever or under-earner.
This requires the ability to see oneself as successful. I don't mean in the way that people often imagine, like winning the jackpot or having someone appear and change your life. The sort that involves establishing goals, overcoming obstacles, knocking on doors, and obtaining better employment. Do not allow unpaid activities to interfere. Make completing your life objectives your primary rehabilitation activity, at least for the time being.

Break free of your regular habits
The issue for porn addicts often has a lot to do with being stuck in a rut. Typically, this takes the shape of a daily pattern that reliably concludes with sitting in front of a computer and a pornographic website. There are many different types of ruts, but the one that comes to mind as the archetype is the one that involves someone who spends all of his free time hanging out at Starbucks and admiring beautiful ladies he

can't have. After that, you spend a lonely evening at home watching online porn.
Whatever your situation, it undoubtedly makes you feel helpless and unable to meet your demands, which drives you to use porn. I am quite certain that most adamant porn addicts need to drastically alter their routine and keep changing it to stop using it.

Take back the concept of a healthy relationship.
The most significant change a porn addict can make is certainly this one. Most sex addicts are unfamiliar with what constitutes a good personal connection. Making new decisions and putting them into practice helps to recover individuals and become stronger at intimacy and relationship skills.
But a lot of porn addicts seem to have abandoned the concept of being in a committed romantic relationship, whether deliberately or subconsciously. They believe it to be too tough or impossible to discover the ideal candidate.
Imagine a realistic image of what a fulfilling relationship might look like for you in this circumstance. This implies that it involves a fulfilling sexual life, therefore you must also consider that. Realistically.

Creating a new sort of life
When you start experiencing significant, positive changes in your life and way of thinking, you will know you have overcome your problem with porn. Your best buddy is a new behavior. Be kind to yourself, yet persistent in making adjustments and changing the way things are done. Above all, notice when your mind starts to revert to the past.

Overcoming a porn **addiction**

There are so many things you could do instead of watching porn, and I'm willing to bet they'd all be more satisfied and give you what you want rather than just a little escape. So why are you still waiting?

Put your gadget to sleep and write down everything for which you are thankful.

• Read your favorite passage from the Bible, mantra, or proverb. Having this on hand could be a smart idea.

• Find a companion and watch a nice movie!

• Address a letter to the cosmos, God, your "higher self," and the planet.

Play a musical instrument. I've got a sizzling date with a small girl named Clarinet, as my friend Squidward puts it. Maybe it's time to learn how to play one if you don't already.

• Compassionately write a letter or card to yourself. Read it aloud to yourself whenever you feel upset.

• Recognize your feelings at the moment. I know. amazing fun however gravely You probably won't be able to stop using porn to suppress or numb your emotions until you deal with them head-on.

• Stretch!

• Take your nieces and nephews to a nearby apple orchard or pumpkin farm.

• Take a seat outdoors and observe the clouds.

• Take up dancing.

• Visit a rock climbing gym and start being foolish while working out hard.

• Attend a sporting event.

• Find a companion by looking for concerts taking place tonight.
• Participate in a sport that you can't perform by yourself, like catch or miniature golf.
• Play catch or kick a soccer ball around with your children or a buddy.
• While you're out on a stroll, working in the yard, or having lunch, listen to an episode of a podcast. There are a ton of informative, interesting podcasts available for free. It may be enlightening and open up new interests for you.
• Shave your hair.
• Start planning the home of your dreams.
• Pray or reflect.
• Go to a tourist spot in your hometown. Imagine yourself in a different town, seeing your current one through fresh eyes. Write a poem, take images, and let it somehow capture your attention. whatever the form of tourism may take.
• Invest 30 minutes in foreign language practice. Start learning one if you don't already know one.
• Whistle or sing.
• Compose a narrative about you or another person.
• Make a list of the traits you respect most about the individuals you admire, followed by the traits you already share with them. Pick 1 thing you'd want to share with them that you don't already. Think about one thing you can do right now to align yourself more with that attribute.
• Create a list of 10 things you want to accomplish before you pass away or 10 things you want to do with your children before you pass away. Start preparing for one.
• Address a letter to a person who has had a gratifying effect on you. Thank you. Post it.

• Play loud music in your room or the living room and jive about. Pull anybody who sees you in to join if they do.
• Unwind on a hammock while reading or doing art.
• Consider a fear you wish you could conquer; realize that the greatest approach to conquer fears is to confront them; develop a strategy for doing so; and immediately take the first step.
• Visit a mall and observe the shoppers.
• Take your children to the park or an ice cream shop.
• Enjoy ice cream outside.
• Visit the theater to see whatever is playing next.
• Engage in interactive play with your pet, take your dog to a dog park, or use someone else's dog.
• Sign up for a local theater company and begin acting. Change into a different character who doesn't object to porn when the trigger occurs.
• Take a bath, but don't use any devices in the room (music exception).
• Enroll in a class at a nearby institution.
• Encourage a grin.
• Read a favorite book or poetry that is always uplifting.
Perform a problem. Maybe it's dorky, but it can also be intriguing and puzzling.
• Visit a museum.
• Start a blog to document your transition away from porn. Reading this would be helpful for so many individuals.
• Purchase a pedicure.
• File off your nails. If you can paint nails, do so.
• Visit the store.
• Take a ride on a motorbike.

• Hand wash your own or another person's vehicle, or take it to a car wash and enjoy some nice music while it's being cleaned.

• Make a dessert and invite a guest over.

• Do you still like the kind of art that you loved before having a laptop and a job? Pick up on whatever creative thought you had when you were 14 again.

• Take a bicycle ride.

• Take a jog. Imagine while you run that your issue, whatever it may be, is being resolved incrementally as your feet touch the ground.

• Take in a sunset or dawn. Seriously! How often have you sat and observed the colors change, despite the cliché? Do it while snuggling, ideally with a cup of hot chocolate. You underestimate how great it is in real life.

• Learn a wild new adventure activity like canyoneering, paragliding, surfing, or whitewater rafting. If you've always wanted to, you probably will. There is no time like the present to get going!

• Work on a project that you have. You are aware of the ones I mean. Maintaining a list of tasks to take on when the trigger appears could be beneficial.

• Create a playlist of fresh songs to listen to. To prevent temptation, you may need to do this task in a busy environment.

• Make a playlist to aid you if you get re-triggered. You may listen to it while biking, walking, running, or any other activity.

• Take a little stroll. Is there anything that even a short stroll won't assist with?

•Take a pal out for a cup of tea or coffee.

- Speak to or text a buddy.
- Invite someone you want to get to know better to hang out with you.
- Make a tasty supper.

And last, be kind to yourself. Whatever you're going through is tough, and I can tell you care about it since you're reading this. That is crucial. There is always hope for us.

www.ingramcontent.com/pod-product-compliance
Lightning Source LLC
LaVergne TN
LVHW050341160826
845677LV00014B/3733

* 9 7 9 8 3 6 8 2 1 4 8 2 5 *